CZERNY

24 EASY STUDIES FOR THE LEFT HAND

OPUS 718
FOR THE PIANO

EDITED BY MAURICE HINSON

AN ALFRED MASTERWORK EDITION

Second Edition
Copyright © MMV by Alfred Music
All rights reserved. Produced in USA.

Cover art: The Old Burgtheater in Vienna, *1783*
by Carl Schütz (Austrian, 1745–1800)
Colored etching
Historisches Museum Stadt Wien, Vienna, Austria
Erich Lessing / Art Resource, New York

CARL CZERNY
24 Easy Studies for the Left Hand, Op. 718

This edition is dedicated to Dr. Pauline Riddle with admiration and appreciation.

Maurice Hinson

Edited by Maurice Hinson

CONTENTS

Foreword

Carl Czerny was born in Vienna on February 20, 1791. After early instruction by his pianist father, he appeared in public as a child prodigy in 1800. Subsequently he became a student of Beethoven and by the age of 15, he had established himself as a respected piano teacher. Among his artist pupils were Theodor Döhler, Sigismond Thalberg, Theodor Kullak, Alfred Jaëll and Franz Liszt. His nonetude works comprise over 300 graduals and offertories, as well as symphonies, masses, writings in music history and theoretical treatises; his opus numbers are near the one-thousand figure. Czerny's one planned international concert tour was cancelled because of the Napoleonic Wars. He died in Vienna on July 15, 1857.

Czerny's talent was remarkable: within a narrow harmonic scheme he developed a prodigious understanding of finger movements possible on the keyboard. He composed many volumes of studies that feature rapid, feathery, well-articulated passages, mainly for the right hand. His style was smooth, pretty and ear-tickling when played fast; he was very popular during his lifetime.

Czerny's Op. 718 is a set of 24 studies that emphasize training of the left hand. The work is not a collection of left-hand solo studies as one might guess from the title, though it focuses on the dexterity of the left hand. The studies include the following types of technique: scales, double thirds, full (four-note) chords, arpeggios, skips, melody and accompaniment in the left-hand part, turns, staccato 16ths, passing of the second finger over the first, fast repeated notes with changing fingers, an exercise to strengthen the fourth and fifth fingers, grace notes and octaves.

Op. 718 and the *School of the Left Hand* (*Schule der linken Hand*), Op. 399, are Czerny's only two opus numbers devoted exclusively to developing the left hand.

24 Easy Studies
for the
Left Hand

Carl Czerny
Op. 718

ⓐ Since this opus focuses mainly on the left-hand part, special attention should be given to it when practicing.

ⓑ The eighths should be heard above the sixteenths.

4

Allegro moderato

2.

ⓐ In order to play clearly the double notes so that they are heard simultaneously, not one after the other, the fingers should first touch the keys and then descend quickly.

ⓑ

ⓒ Grace notes performed with the time-value of the note.

ⓓ Play very light using only the wrist.

ⓐ The upper-voice melody should be predominant, while the left-hand accompaniment should be very light, but clear.

ⓐ Play skips here and on the following page slowly at first, until they can be made with certainty.

8

ⓐ There should not be a break between these notes.

10

ⓐ The notes written as eighths must be emphasized, but played somewhat lighter than the melody of the upper voice.

8.

ⓐ Staccato, from the knuckle joint.

Allegretto vivace

ⓐ The hand should be kept as still as possible in these figures.

14

(a) Additional practice may be needed so the second finger passes smoothly over the first in these passages.

Allegretto scherzoso

12.

ⓐ As a preparatory exercise, play these measures with strong execution:

ⓑ Practice as in Study 2.

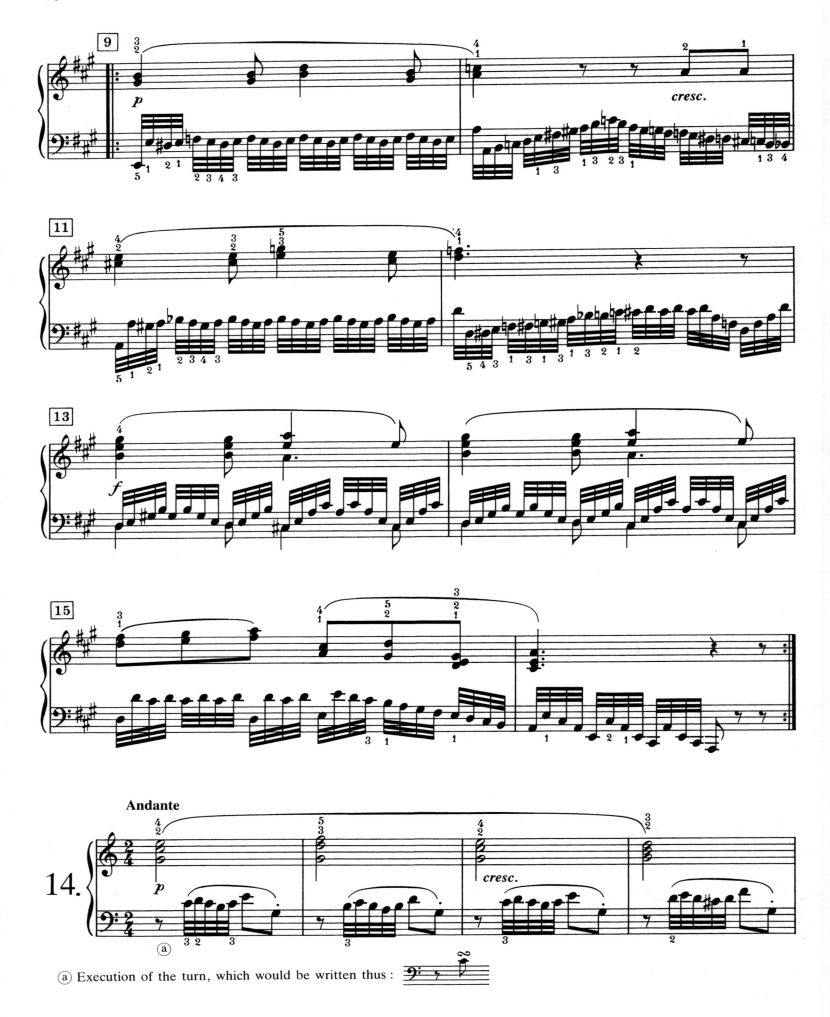

(a) Execution of the turn, which would be written thus:

(b) When repeating notes on a single key, the hand moves left with each change of the finger.

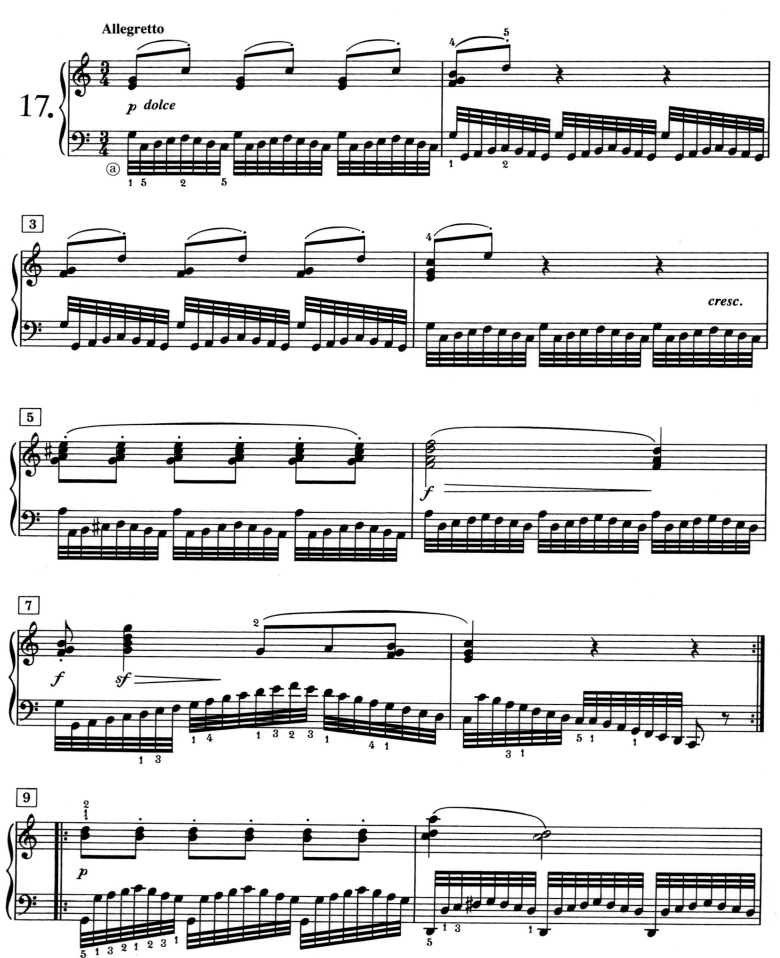

ⓐ This is an excellent exercise to strengthen the fourth and fifth fingers.

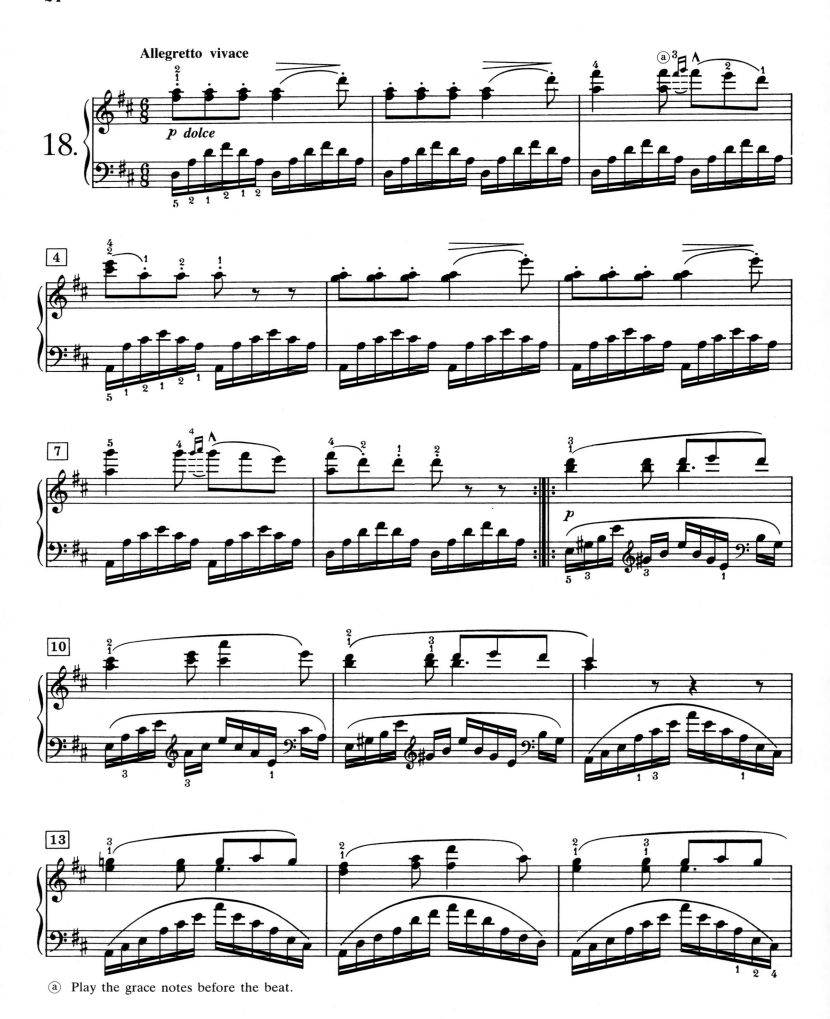

ⓐ Play the grace notes before the beat.

28

Allegro commodo

21.

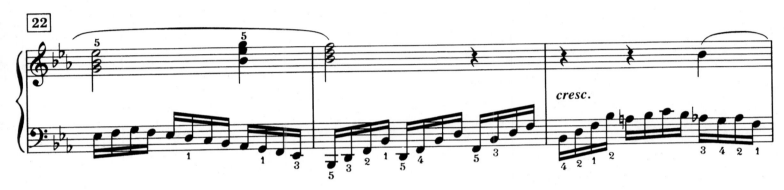

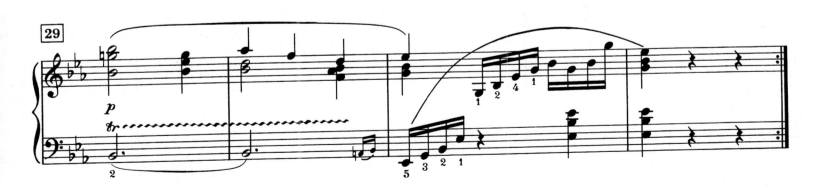

Ⓒ **End trill on Ab:**

Allegro vivace

24.

ⓐ Do not play this exercise too often in succession with the left hand, as it may strain the wrist. As soon as the least fatigue is felt, stop playing.